3.50

Kids Working with Computers

THE IBM® LOGO MANUAL

Thomas Milton Kemnitz   Lynne Mass
Joseph Kuffler   Michael Rubin   Debbie Toll

CHILDRENS PRESS™
CHICAGO

IBM® is a registered trademark of International Business Machines Corp. There is no affiliation between International Business Machines Corp. and the publisher of this book, and neither this book nor its contents are sponsored, authorized, or approved by International Business Machines Corp.

Library of Congress Cataloging in Publication Data
Main entry under title:

The IBM LOGO manual.

(Kids working with computers)
On t.p. the registered trademark symbol ''R'' is superscript following ''IBM'' in the title.
Includes index.
Summary: Explains how to use the computer language LOGO to write fundamental programs for IBM microcomputers.
1. LOGO (Computer program [redacted]puters—Programming—
Juvenile literature. [1. IBM micro[redacted]ogram language)
3. Programming (Computers) [redacted]

QA76.73.L63I26 1985 001.64'24 85-5279
ISBN 0-516-08427-5 (lib. bdg.)

Library bound edition published by Childrens Press under license from Trillium Press.

Printed in the United States of America.

1 2 3 4 5 6 7 8 9 10 R 94 93 92 91 90 89 88 87 86 85

CONTENTS

1

Introduce Yourself to LOGO

Let's get to know our computer. To start:

1. Put the LOGO disk in the disk drive (IBM® disk from LOGO Computer Systems, Inc.).
2. Close the door of the disk drive.
3. Turn on your monitor, computer, etc.
4. You will see these words:

```
A> DATE
CURRENT DATE IS TUE 1-01-1980
ENTER NEW DATE:
```

Then press ↵. The screen will show:

```
A> TIME
CURRENT TIME IS 0:00:08.89
ENTER NEW TIME:
```

Press ↵. Eventually you will see:

```
WELCOME TO LOGO
?□
```

The question mark is called the **prompt.** The blinking white box is called the **cursor.**

If you have your own **initialized disk**, remove LOGO and insert your own disk so that you may save programs. See the Glossary for instructions on initializing.

2

Meet the Turtle

What can your turtle do? Your LOGO turtle can move forward, back, right, and left. When given as commands, these directions have abbreviations:

FORWARD	FD
BACK	BK
RIGHT	RT
LEFT	LT

Then you can get him to stand on his head! Let's find out how to do this.

In order to meet your turtle, type:

```
SHOWTURTLE
  or
HOME
```

3

Turtle Colors

Can turtle drawings be colorful? Yes! If you have a color monitor, you can have both a background color and a pencolor. The background colors are:

0 BLACK	6 BROWN	11 LIGHT CYAN
1 BLUE	7 WHITE	12 LIGHT RED
2 GREEN	8 GRAY	13 LIGHT MAGENTA
3 CYAN	9 LIGHT BLUE	14 YELLOW
4 RED	10 LIGHT GREEN	15 HIGH-INTENSITY WHITE
5 MAGENTA		

To change the background color, type SETBG with the number of the color you want.

To change pencolor, type SETPAL to 0 or 1 and type SETPC to the color you want.

COLOR	PALETTE 0	PALETTE 1
0	SAME AS BACKGROUND	
1	GREEN	CYAN
2	RED	MAGENTA
3	BROWN	WHITE

You can also use shortcut codes for background and pencolors. Try this:

```
?SETBG 11
?SETPC 0
?FD 45
?RT 45
?FD 45
?RT 45
?FD 45
```

What did you see? **SETBG** is the shortcut for "Set Background Color." **SETPC** is the shortcut for "Set Pencolor."

If you have been enjoying color, try a few experiments if you want the original colors. For example, type:

```
SETPAL 1
SET PC 3
SET BG 0
CS
```

We like SETBG 11.

Now try experimenting with your own color programs.

4

Print a Message

LOGO does more than graphics. This lesson and the next one will give you a brief introduction to words (text) and numbers.

Try this by typing exactly what you see:

```
PRINT [HELLO THERE]
```

Push **ENTER**. What do you see?

Try it with your own message.

LOGO has a clever way for you to invent your own program—it is called a **procedure** in turtle-talk. Try this. Type the following:

```
?TO SING  ← First type TO and the title.
>PRINT [OPEN MOUTH] } Then type the steps in your procedure.
>PRINT [LA-LA-LA]   }
>END  ←Then type END.
```

LOGO will say **SING DEFINED**. Now every time you want the steps in the procedure "Sing," just type SING and press ENTER. Try it.

This is called *defining a procedure.* When you see the symbol >, it reminds you that you are defining a procedure. **END** signals that you have finished a procedure. **CLEARTEXT** clears the text from the screen.

If you want to repeat a procedure, try this:

```
?REPEAT 5 [SING]
```

What happens?

How could you run this procedure 1,000 times? Try it. To stop, press **BREAK.**

5

Mr. Turtle's Math Magic

LOGO has easy ways to do math. Try this:

```
?PR 10 + 9
```

Now push ENTER. What do you see?

Now try these. Don't forget to press ENTER after each line.

```
?PR 20 - 10
?PR 10 * 11
?PR 18/9
```

Can you figure out which sign is for addition? subtraction? multiplication? division?

Try out your own ideas.

6

How to SAVE and LOAD

If you want to **SAVE** a procedure, do this:

1. Remove the LOGO disk from the disk drive.
2. Insert an initialized disk (see Glossary).
3. Type `?SAVE` and the procedure title, putting a single set of quotation marks only before the name of the program:

   ```
   ?SAVE ''SING
   ```

   The red light on the disk drive will go on, and the monitor will tell you the procedure was saved.

NOTE: SAVE will save every procedure in memory, so be sure that the procedure you want to save is the only one in memory.

If you have saved a procedure on disk—or you want another procedure—type **CATALOG** to see the names of the procedures on the disk. Find the name you want, and type LOAD with a space, quotation marks, and the name of the procedure, like this:

```
?LOAD ''SING
```

Then just type the title and the procedure will RUN.

7

A Procedure from Mr. Turtle

To teach the LOGO turtle how to write a **program** (a procedure), you type the word TO and some step-by-step instructions. For example, you can write a procedure for a square. Try this:

```
?TO   SQUARE  ←First type TO and the title.
>FD   40
>RT   90
>FD   40
>RT   90
>FD   40      Then type the steps in your procedure.
>RT   90
>FD   40
>RT   90
>END          ←Then type END.
```

The **monitor** (screen) will say:

```
SQUARE DEFINED
```

Once you have defined a procedure, the computer's memory will not let you use that name for a different square unless you **erase (ER)** the memory by typing:

```
?ER ''SQUARE.
```

Now you can define SQUARE in a different way. For example, a shorter way to do the same SQUARE is:

```
?TO SQUARE
>REPEAT 4 [FD 40 RT 90]
>END
```

What does the screen say? How can you SAVE your SQUARE? You are correct if you typed:

```
?SAVE ''SQUARE
```

You can use your SQUARE procedure as a command, over and over. Try this:

```
?SQUARE
?FD 10
?SQUARE
```

What happens?

 Experiment with many SQUARES.

8

The Printer

If you have a printer and want to keep track of your ideas while you are experimenting, turn on the printer and type the following:

```
SAVE ''LPT1
         ↑
```

This is the input that makes the printer work.

To stop the printer, type:

```
CLOSE ''LPT1
```

To SAVE just one procedure, type:

```
SAVE ''LPT1
```

Now LOAD your SQUARE procedure and try this:

```
?TO SQUAREWHEEL
>REPEAT 12 [RT 45 SQUARE]
>RT 30
>REPEAT 12 [RT 45 SQUARE]
>RT 30
>REPEAT 12 [RT 45 SQUARE]
>END
```

Change the procedure in different ways and see what designs you get.

Do you want to keep a record of everything as you do it? Type:

```
DRIBBLE ''LPT1
```

NOTE: This will work only with a parallel printer.

9

Hide and Seek

It sometimes gets boring watching the turtle move in every direction. The command **HIDETURTLE** or **HT** will make drawing on the screen faster. It hides the turtle! Try this:

```
?ST
?REPEAT 4 [RT 90 FD 50]
```

Before going to the next step, type **CLEAN**.

Now try this:

```
?HT
?REPEAT 4 [RT 90 FD 50]
```

Did you notice that the lines were drawn faster the second time you did this?

Now add colors to get a nice procedure. (ST returns the turtle).

10

Can I Draw My Face?

Drawing a face on paper is easy. It can be easy in LOGO, too. All you have to do is to be able to lift up the pen and put it down again. You can do this with these commands:

PENUP (PU)

PENDOWN (PD)

Now try this:

```
?RT 90 FD 15
?PU
?FD 15
?PD
?FD 15
```

Did you draw two lines for eyes?

Try to add a nose and a mouth.

Add colors.

Review

What do these mean:

SETBG

SETPC

HT

ST

11

Mr. Turtle's Merry-go-round

Have you thought about drawing a circle? It is very easy. All you have to do is use your **REPEAT** command. Try this:

```
REPEAT 360 [RT 1 FD 1]
```

What happened? Why do you think you put 360 after the command REPEAT?

Now that you have made a circle, you are ready to learn an easier way to do it.

12

Easy Circles

Try this:

```
LOAD ''TOOLS
```

To get a circle, type:

```
CIRCLER 30
    or
CIRCLEL 30
```

The number 30 is the **radius** of the circle. The L stands for "left." The command CIRCLEL turns the circle to the left.

How could you turn a circle to the right with a radius of 50?

When you draw circles from TOOLS, each circle must have an **input.** In this case, the input is the radius. Now look at what the input is for **arcs.** Try this:

```
ARCR 30 100
```

or

```
ARCL 30 100
```

The first number (30) is the radius. The second number (100) is the distance in degrees around the edge.

Experiment. Make a face.

Review

1. What does REPEAT do?
2. What are [ ] for?

13

The Egg Timer, or Delays

Train your turtle to slow down with the command **WAIT.** Try this:

```
TO HOLD
>CS
?FD 50
?RT 90
?FD 50
?WAIT 100
?FD 50
```

What happened?

See if you can make up some procedures with the command **WAIT**.

14

Idea Time...Fun with LOGO

You have learned a lot so far, so let's have fun. Here are some ideas. If you have made a procedure for SQUARE, LOAD it and type:

```
?TO MANYSQUARE
>REPEAT 4 [RT 90 SQUARE]
>END
```

Now try this:

```
LOAD ''STARTUP
```

Then type:

```
?TO SQUARE.CIRCLE
>SQUARE
>CIRCLER 50
>END
```

This may also be typed:

```
?TO SQUARE.CIRCLE
>SQUARE CIRCLER 50
>END
```

What is the difference between the two procedures?

15

ERASEFILE

Do you have a program that you want to take off the disk? If you do, type:

```
ERASEFILE ''TITLE
```

This is helpful if you have a procedure you want to change and then SAVE. After you LOAD your procedure and change it, **ERASEFILE** the name and then SAVE the procedure again.

16

The Fixer...Editing

If you make a mistake while writing a procedure, don't worry. It is easy to fix. Suppose you typed this:

```
?TO ME
>FD 45
>RT 90
>FD 45
>RT 90
>FD 45
>RT 90
>FD 25 ←OOPS! You meant to put 45.
>RT 90
>END
```

To correct the mistake, type:

?EDIT ME or ?ED ''ME

You will see:

```
TO ME
FD 45
RT 90
FD 45
RT 90
FD 45
RT 90
FD 25
RT 90
END
LOGO EDITOR
```

Now you can correct your mistake by pressing the ↓ until you are on the line with 25 and then the ← until you are over the 2. Then press **DEL**. This erases your error. Press **ESCAPE** when you are finished editing.

17

Command Your Computer

COMMAND	WHAT COMMAND DOES
?PO ''TITLE	prints out the steps in the procedure
?POTS	prints out all the titles of procedures in the memory
?POPS	prints out the steps of all procedures in the memory
?ER ''TITLE	erases the procedure from the memory
?ERASEFILE ''TITLE	erases the procedure from the disk and catalog
?ERPS	erases all procedures from the memory
?HT	hides the turtle
?ST	shows the turtle
CTRL-W	stops the procedure temporarily; hit any key to continue
CTRL-S	splits the screen—part turtle, part words
CTRL-T	makes the whole screen use words (full text)
CTRL-L	makes the whole screen graphics (all turtle, no words)

18

Erasable Pen

Do you have an erasable pen? Now you can have an erasable turtle!

Suppose you had intended to type:

```
?FD 30
?RT 45
?FD 18
```

Instead you accidentally typed this and pressed the RETURN key:

```
?FD 30
?RT 45
?FD 180
```

You could type:

```
?PENERASE or (PE)
?BK 180
?PD
?FD 18
```

Or you could use **PX—PENREVERSE**—here. It reverses the color of everything the turtle crosses.

Try either way. Is everything OK now?

19

Has Your Turtle Lost His Way?

If your turtle has lost its way and you can't see in what direction it is heading, type:

```
?PR HEADING
```

LOGO will respond with a number such as 180. This means that the turtle is pointing 180° away from straight up, which is 0.

The drawing shows how a circle would look if you traced it around the outside edge for 360°.

What if LOGO answered 270°? Where would the turtle be pointing?

How could you turn the turtle to 0°?

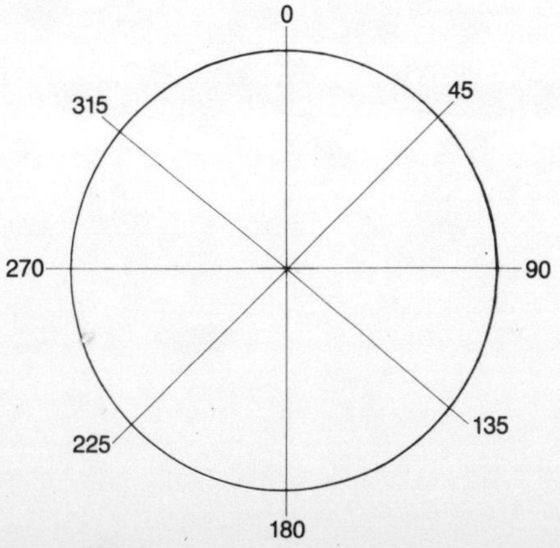

20

Turn the Turtle

You have already learned that you can turn the turtle by typing RT or LT and the number of degrees you want to turn. You can also turn the turtle with another simple command—**SETHEADING** or **SETH**.

Suppose the turtle is pointing straight down (toward 180°) and you want it to point straight up. Look at the circle on page 31. What number is straight up? If you type **SETH 0** what will happen? Try it.

How could you point the turtle to the right 135°?

If you want to return the turtle to the center of the screen facing 0°, type **HOME.**

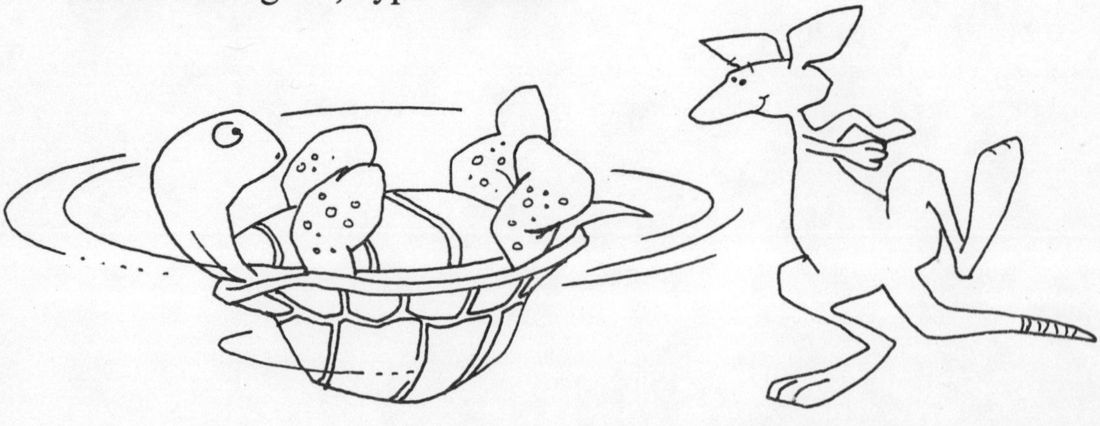

21

FENCE, WINDOW, WRAP

Type the following:

```
?SETH 11
?FENCE
?FD 150
```

What happens?

Now type:

```
?WINDOW
?FD 1000
```

What happens?

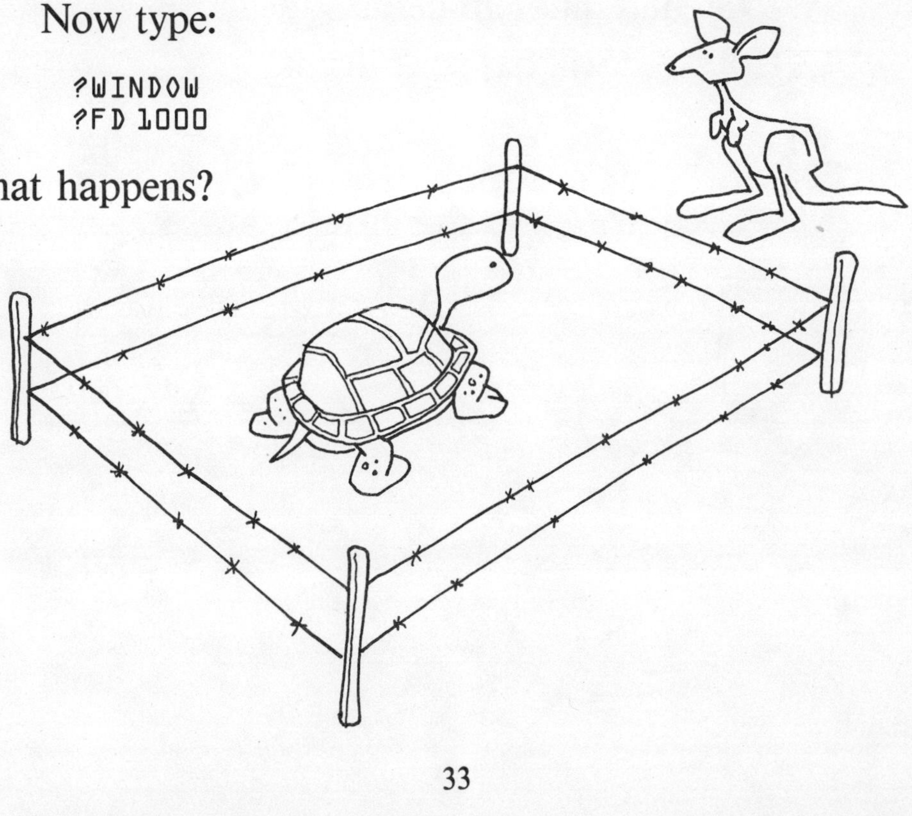

FENCE will put a fence around the screen so the turtle cannot go off the screen. **WINDOW** will let the turtle out of the fence, but it cannot get in the other side because that side has a fence and no window.

Now type:

```
?WRAP
?FD 1000
```

What happens? **WRAP** will get rid of both the window and the fence.

Try experimenting with FENCE, WINDOW, WRAP, and different inputs.

22

Follow the Dots

The command **DOT** will place a dot on the screen without moving the turtle. Try this:

Location of
X-coordinate
↓

```
?DOT [80 5]
?FD 10    ↑
?FENCE    Location of Y-coordinate
?RT 90
?FD 180
?WINDOW
?FD 180
?WRAP
```

The **X-coordinate** is a horizontal position. The **Y-coordinate** is a vertical position.

If you type **PR XCOR**, you will find the position of the X-coordinate. What do you think the command **PR YCOR** does?

23

PR PEN

When you type **PR PEN,** LOGO will tell you what your pen position is, as well as the pencolor number. Try typing this:

```
?FD 70
?PU RT 90
?FD 10
?PR PEN
```

LOGO will tell you **PENUP 3.**

Depending upon what has been typed, LOGO might respond with:

```
PENUP (PU)
PENDOWN (PD)
PENREVERSE (PX)
PENERASE (PE)
```

24

Dumping Your Picture to the Printer

To dump a high-resolution graphics screen to the printer, type:

```
SAVEPIC. ''LPT1
?SQUAREWHEEL
?SAVEPIC ''LPT1
```

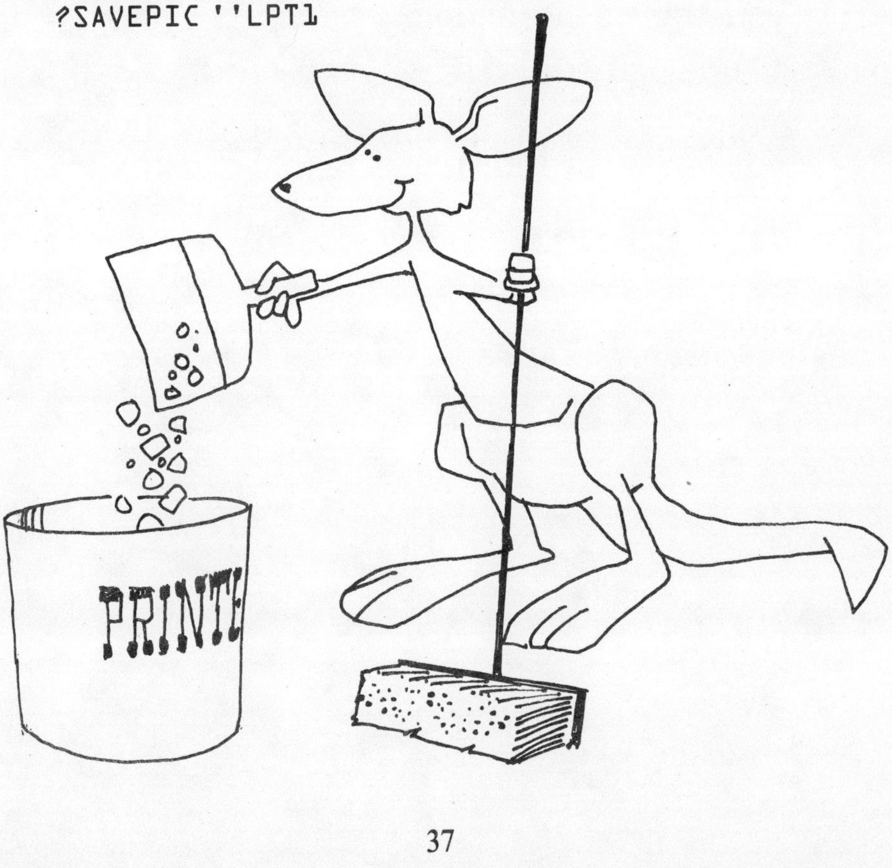

25

Squashed Circles

If you want to try some funny-looking circles, LOAD **"TOOLS** and try these tricks. Type:

```
?.SETSCRUNCH .25
?CIRCLER 20
```

← *SETCRUNCH always has a period . before it.*

What happened?

If you want a normal-looking circle, type:

```
?.SETSCRUNCH .8
```

Experiment with different numbers with **SETSCRUNCH**.

26

PR .SCRUNCH

If you have been experimenting with SETSCRUNCH and forget what the "scrunch" is set to, you can ask your computer by typing **PR .SCRUNCH.** Here is an example:

```
?.SETSCRUNCH .4
?FD 7
?RT 7
?LOAD ''AIDS
FILE NOT FOUND
?CIRCLEL 5
?PR .SCRUNCH
.4
```
← *Notice that the computer tells you the scrunch.*

27

MANYSHAPES...
Changing Squares

In lesson 7, you learned how to make a square. But suppose you wanted to be able to change the size of a square easily. Try this:

```
?TO SQUARE :SIDE
>REPEAT 4 [FD :SIDE RT 90]
>END
```

Now using that procedure, try this:

```
?SQUARE 40
?SQUARE 10
?SQUARE 20
?SQUARE 30
```

There are endless variations using inputs. You can create many shapes. Try this:

```
?TO MANYSHAPES :SIDE :ANGLE
>FD :SIDE
>RT :ANGLE
>MANYSHAPES :SIDE + 3 :ANGLE
>END
```

Experiment with different inputs such as:

```
?MANYSHAPES 6 97
```

When you have seen enough, hit CTRL G.

Try other numbers.

Here are some examples of MANYSHAPES that other children have invented:

Title	**Inputs for MANYSHAPES**	
Star	1	150
Rose	5	94
Doily	1	170
Maze	3	45
Better. Stairs	53	243
Endless.Tunnel	8	90

28

SETX
SETY

In lesson 22, **PR XCOR** and **PR YCOR** were discussed. If you want to set the position of the X-coordinate, type **SETX** with a plus (+) for right or a minus (−) for left and a number. Try this:

```
?SETX + 50
```

The Y-coordinate goes up and down.

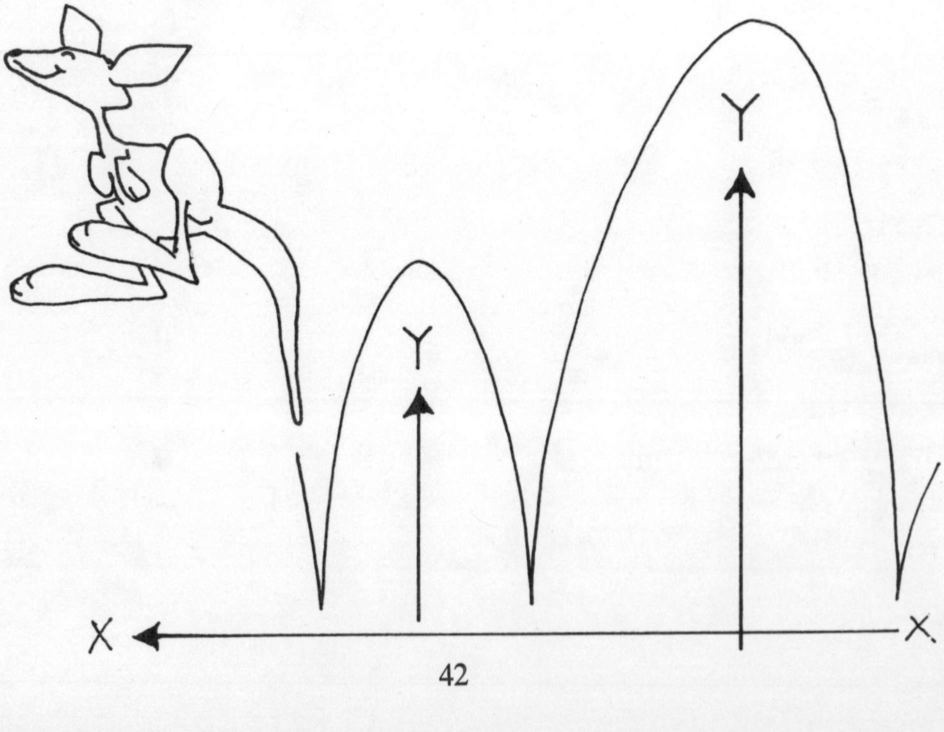

GLOSSARY

BOOT To load a program into a computer from a diskette.

BRACKETS Two half squares ([ ]). You get these on the screen by pushing SHIFT + N or M.

CLEAN A command that erases graphics but nothing else.

CLEARSCREEN (CS) A command that erases everything you have drawn on the screen.

CLEARTEXT A command that tells the computer to erase all text (words) from the screen (if you are not in the graphics mode).

COMMAND Information you enter that tells the computer what to do; for example, SETBG, SETPC, TO, etc.

CURSOR The white blinking square that moves on the screen. It shows where the next character will be printed and moves one space ahead of whatever you are writing.

DISK Stores information magnetically.

DISK DRIVE "Reads" the disk and converts its information to electrical impulses to be used by the computer.

DUMP A command that draws your LOGO design on the printer (it works only on the dot-matrix printer).

EDIT (ED) A command that puts you into the LOGO editor.

ENTER Pushing this key enables you to go to the next line. It also processes whatever has been typed into the computer.

ERASE (ER) A command that erases a program from the memory.

ERASEFILE A command that erases a program from the disk.

ERPS A command that erases all procedures from the memory.

FENCE A command that does not allow the turtle to go off the screen.

HIDETURTLE (HT) A command that makes the turtle disappear.

HOME A command that puts the turtle in the center of the screen pointing straight up (0°).

INITIALIZED DISK A disk that is prepared for use. A disk can be initialized by booting another disk and then typing INIT HELLO.

INPUT Requires the user to type in a number after a word command when the word is followed by a space and a colon. For example, in a procedure such as SQUARE :SIDE, the :SIDE indicates the need for a number to tell the computer how long to make the side.

LOAD A command that allows you to load a procedure from the disk to the computer.

OUTPUT What you see on the screen, printer, or other hardware.

PENDOWN (PD) A command that enables the turtle to move while drawing. The opposite of PENUP.

PENERASE (PE) A command that erases lines drawn by the turtle.

PENREVERSE (PX) A command that reverses the color of anything the pen crosses.

PENUP (PU) A command that enables the turtle to move without drawing. The opposite of PENDOWN.

PO A command that prints out a procedure.

POPS A command that prints out all procedures in the memory.

POTS A command that prints out the titles of all procedures that are in the memory.

PR HEADING A command that prints on the screen the degrees (to the right of vertical) that the turtle is heading.

PRINT (PR) A command that must be entered before writing a statement. For example, PR [HELLO] allows the computer to display HELLO on the screen after you push RETURN.

PRINTER An output machine that has paper and prints a hardcopy of what you command it to print, such as a procedure (PO "TITLE) or a picture (DUMP).

PROCEDURE Instructions to the computer telling it what to do and how to do it. A procedure can be recalled from disk or memory whenever that procedure is needed.

PROMPT The sign at the beginning of a line (either a ? or a >).

PR PEN A command that prints the color of the pen and tells whether it is in the up, down, reverse, or erase position.

PR SCRUNCH A command that prints out what the scrunch is, such as .8

REPEAT A command that tells the computer to repeat your commands. You must tell the computer how many times to repeat the command.

RESET (or CTRL-RESET) The key at the top right of the keyboard. Hitting this key will disrupt LOGO. To get back into LOGO, type ST or CATALOG.

RETURN Pushing this key enables you to go to the next line. It also processes whatever has been typed into the computer.

SAVE A command that allows you to save your procedures on the disk.

SETBACKGROUND (SETBG) A command that lets you change the color of the background of the screen.

SETHEADING (SETH) A command that sets the turtle's angle in degrees (from 0 to 360).

SETPENCOLOR (SETPC) A command that lets you change the color of the pen with which the turtle draws.

SETSCRUNCH A command that will change the shape of a circle.

SHOWTURTLE (ST) A command that places the turtle in the middle of the screen. It puts you in the graphics (drawing) mode.

STARTUP A procedure that contains circles and arcs. It is also referred to as "STARTUP" AIDS.

WAIT A command that allows a procedure to pause.

X-COORDINATE A horizontal position on the screen as measured from a central line.

Y-COORDINATE A vertical position on the screen as measured from a central line.

ERRORS

Sometimes you may try out ideas and discover that the computer cannot do what you want it to do. When this happens, you will see an error message. Here are some examples:

PROGRAM IS ALREADY DEFINED	You have tried to save a program that already exists. If you decide to change it, erase the title with ERASEFILE.
NUMBER TOO BIG	You have typed a number that is too big for LOGO. Try a smaller number.
I'M HAVING TROUBLE WITH THE DISK	You may have tried to SAVE without a disk. Try again.
CAN'T DIVIDE BY ZERO	Mr. Turtle dropped out of school so he cannot divide by zero.
DISK FULL	You have filled up your disk. Initialize a new one.

One error you should worry about if you see it is !!! LOGO SYSTEM BUG !!! If this occurs, write to LOGO Computer Systems, Inc. For other errors, look at the *IBM® LOGO Reference Manual.*

QUESTIONS AND IDEAS

If you have questions about LOGO or want to share ideas with other LOGO-ites, the National LOGO Exchange is a friendly source. The address is:

The National LOGO Exchange
Tom Lough, Editor
Box 5341
Charlottesville, VA 22905

Another address you might find useful is:

LOGO Computer Systems, Inc.
368 Congress Street
Boston, MA 02210

INDEX